THE
ORGANIZATIONAL
VISIONARY

THE DYNAMICS OF ORGANIZATIONAL
LEADERSHIP

ANDRE THOMAS

GREATNESS
PUBLISHING

www.ignitingworldchangers.org

Published by Greatness Publishing, Ontario, Canada

Cover Design and formatting by Farouk J. Roberts,
Brands & Love Creative
www.brandsnlove.com

Photos by Natalie Ali

Library and Archives Canada

ISBN 978-1-927579-06-0

ACKNOWLEDGMENTS

Special thanks go to:
Nancy Dickerson for editing

I dedicate this book to my Father
Dr Armand Thomas
for teaching me the value of hard work

CONTENTS

INTRODUCTION

The craft of building great organizations is not often the focus of the business and social entrepreneur when they count the cost of accomplishing their visions. It is however, one of the greatest factors that will determine the eventual impact of the business or nonprofit corporation.

Organizations are built because individual visionaries have a solution that cannot be served by them alone. They are compelled to organize people, financial and material resources in a structured and strategic way to accomplish their visions. The art of deploying the skills, character and passion of people while maximizing financial and material resources to create goods and services that add value to humanity is the subject of this book.

I have worked as a strategic and organizational development consultant for the last ten years with governments, large corporations, small businesses, and nonprofit corporations and sports franchises. Some of these organizations have been great and others not so great. They all have DNA just like the human body which determines their potential and effectiveness. Organizational DNA is often created by default and can become the greatest unseen enemy of the growth of the business. Leaders of organizations, because their organizations are essential their own creations, always have a capacity to redesign and recreate the DNA of a dysfunctional organization. I have written this book to equip existing and aspiring organizational visionaries with the wisdom to intentionally create or recreate an organization with a DNA that supports their dreams. It will be divided into two sections.

Section I - The DNA of Great Organizations

Section II – Dynamics of Great Organizational Leadership

PART ONE:

....

THE DNA OF GREAT ORGANIZATIONS

CHAPTER 1

WHAT IS ORGANIZATIONAL DNA?

Man cannot redesign his DNA because he did not create himself. However, organizational visionaries can redesign the DNA of their organization because they created it.

Deoxyribonucleic acid (DNA) is a nucleic acid that contains the genetic codes used in the development and functioning of all known living organisms. It is often compared to a set of blueprints or a recipe, since it contains the instructions needed to construct the other components of cells. It is unseen to the naked eye, yet, it determines the development of all living organisms.

Organizations also have a DNA, made up of nine components:

1. The Solution of the Organization

   Every organization that is viable, strong and growing excels at solving problems in each niche. Simply put, successful organizations solve problems well. The problems that they solve could be as different as Alcoholic Anonymous, a non-profit organization that helps people overcome alcohol addictions, or the Microsoft Corporation that helps people with computer software solutions. When the problem that an organization is suited to solve becomes unclear, the future of the organization is in jeopardy.

2. The Vision of the Organization

   Vision is a clear mental portrait of a preferred future. It is the defined destination point for all great organizations. It acts like a compass which has the effect of a magnet pulling the organization into higher levels of achievements. When vision is unclear in an organization, chaos is inevitable. It's like the human body that is not sure of where it wants to go. The right hand and left foot are moving south and the left foot and left arm are moving north. It creates division which simply means two visions. Some organizations have many different visions operating within them. In some organizations that I have worked with, there have been as many as ten opposing visions of direction operating within its structure. This leads to organizational standstill.

3. The Culture of the Organization

The culture for an organization can be created by design or by default. It is the invisible yet tangible set of values which shape the character of the organization. When those values are good and undergird the vision, the culture of the organization acts like a wind blowing the organization forward. When those values are negative, they act like a weight, slow down, and sometimes drag the organization into failure and financial losses.

4. The Decision-Making Model of the Organization

Decisions determine destiny. An organization, similar to a person, cannot sustain a quality of existence that is greater than the quality of its decisions. You decide your way into sustained success and can decide your way out of failure into victory. Organizations, like people, can have a reactive, emotionally unstable decision making model that does not reflect their vision, reality and their potential. They can have the wrong people making the wrong decision about the right issues.

5. The Financial-Revenue Model of the Organization

Money is the fuel of dreams and revenue generation is the fear of many organizations. An organization that does not constantly optimize its revenue generation model, in accordance with its values, will end up in financial hardships. Money is a medium of exchange of goods and services. Successful entrepreneurs are those who solve problems for others at a profit. Successful social entrepreneurs are those who solve social problems for people, with excellence, in a financially sustainable way.

6. The Leadership Approach of the CEO and the Leadership Team

Every organization will rise and fall on its leader. The primary leader of the organization is truly the ceiling on the realization of the potential of an organization. Primary leaders matter. They set the tone; they are navigators and they, more than any of the members of staff, create the future that the organization will live in. When they are competent and ethical, the climate of the organization is ideal for growth. When they are incompetent and unethical, storms of crisis are a constant occurrence.

7. The Type of People the Organization Attracts

The people in an organization determine its potential. People can initiate and create or stop good things from happening. The collective talent, passion and character of the people of an organization will either have a lifting or a crippling effect on the operations of the organization.

8. The Personnel Structure of the Organization

The structure of a family determines how the family behaves. Similarly, the structure of an organization determines how the organization behaves. To change the behavior of an organization, you must evaluate the authority structure and how it influences behavior.

9. The Operational System of the Organization

The purpose of the system is to make daily, weekly and monthly processes easier. If the processes are not effective, systems of ineffectiveness become an organizational tradition. However, if the processes that make up the system are effective, a tradition of productivity will be the byproduct. Simply stated the system is important.

CHAPTER 2

DEFINE THE ORGANIZATIONAL SOLUTION AND VISION

*Organizations that no longer solve
problems become a problem.*

Organizations that no longer solve problems eventually die. This is because the life blood of an organization is its ability to create a service or provide a product that practically solves problems for enough people to merit its existence. At the core of the DNA of a great organization, is a clear understanding of what problems it is organizing people, finances and material resources to solve. Great organizations only organize to solve problems that they can be number one, number two or at least number three in their particular industry and geographical location.

The definition of the solutions that an organization is going to solve is the cornerstone of organizational development.

When that process arrives at the wrong conclusion, the days of that organization are numbered. There are many reasons why organizational visionaries choose the wrong solution to serve through the vehicle of the organization. I will now examine some of them.

1. Passion for Product or Service That is No Longer Relevant

> Passion is a strong emotion that compels people into action. It is the source of all great accomplishments and has also been the source of some of the greatest organizational start up failures in history. Passion works best when it's married to reality. It produces children called determination, perseverance and energy for accomplishment. When it is not married to reality, it produces a blind optimism that usually ends up in a disaster. I am reminded of an organizational start up in the Island of Barbados, where I lived for ten years. A very passionate business entrepreneur decided to build a five star spa on the Island of Barbados. They decided that

no expense will be spared in creating this awesome SPA. They invested over a million US dollar in creating the dream. And when they launched their business they were bankrupt within six months. Why did this happen? It is very simple, in their passion for their dream, they forgot a brutal reality which was that the citizens of Barbados and its hundreds and thousands of tourists preferred the natural SPA of the Caribbean Sea rather than a SPA modeled after Scandinavian taste. Their passion not married with reality made them blind.

2. Passion to Produce Goods and Services That You do not Understand

Passion can cause you to invest in a business that you do not understand, start a venture without counting the cost, and create a social organization to solve problems that you are unable to solve. When this happens, an organizational visionary becomes a prisoner of the competence and loyalty of staff and is always a few steps from failure. When you start an organization in an area of personal deficiency, you lack leadership intuition, which is necessary i n making quality decisions.

The Organizational Vision

Organizational vision is a clear mental portrait of what the people of an organization maximizing its available resources can produce with distinction, impact and sustainable profit. Organizational vision is the cornerstone of every great organization; when vision is not clear within an organization, chaos is inevitable. An organization works the same way as a human body with the CEO and his board acting as the brain of the organization.

There are three visionary dysfunctions in an organization that I want us to examine:

A. Organizational Coma

When the human brain is not working properly or asleep, the body goes into a coma. The same happens to an organization whose leaders are asleep at the wheel.

B. Organizational Paralysis

When the brain is functioning properly and the nerves that are connected to the rest of the body are severed or not functioning properly, paralysis is the result. This is the same for organizations who are led by vibrant focused leaders surrounded by team members that do not follow instructions with passion or commitment. In these cases, organizational paralysis is the result.

C. Organizational Cancer

When the cells of the human body rebel cancers are formed. The parallel is an organization where individuals and groups within the organizations carve out separate power bases within the organization to promote agendas that are at odds with the organization's leaders and purposes.

The Chrysler Story

On April 30, 2009, Chrysler, LLC, an American iconic company formed in 1925 filed for Chapter 11 bankruptcy protection and announced a plan for a partnership with Italian automaker Fiat. On June 1, Chrysler LLC stated they were selling some assets and operations to the newly formed company Chrysler Group LLC. Fiat will now hold a 20% stake in the new company, with an option to increase this to 35%, and eventually to 51%.

The story of the demise of Chrysler and the rise of the Big Asian Four -Toyota, Honda, Nissan, and Hyundai, is a story of missed opportunities and not adapting to the changing needs of the American Car consumer. Chrysler, the recipient of two government bailouts in 1979 and 2008/2009 worth nearly ten billion dollars at this time of writing did not make the changes to its cars, culture, structure, processes and systems to retain its position as a leading player in the worldwide car industry, This story must serve as a warning for all organizational visionaries that failure to meet the needs of your chosen market with distinction will lead to extinction if not corrected at the root.

Exercises:

Give an example of an organization that has been in existence for over twenty years and still relevant and growing because it continually adapts itself to provide goods and services that meet the current needs of its market.

_____

_____

_____

_____

_____

_____

_____

_____

_____

Give an example of a business or social organization that was a market leader in their industry that is no longer in existence because it did not adapt to meet the changing needs of its clients or match the emerging new technology and trends.

_____

_____

_____

_____

_____

_____

_____

_____

_____

What are the needs that your organization can meet using its available resources and be first, second or third in your market area and why?

_____

_____

_____

_____

_____

_____

_____

_____

_____

Write out a vision statement for your organization that is reflective of what your organization, while maximizing available people, finances, and materials, can produce with distinction and sustained revenue.

_____

_____

_____

_____

_____

_____

_____

_____

CHAPTER 3

DEFINE THE CULTURE THAT SUPPORTS THE ACHIEVEMENT OF THE VISION

*The culture of an organization is
its best friend or worst enemy.*

Culture can be defined as the way of life of a people. It sets the climate for an organization. It can be created by default or by design. In my work, I've noticed that organizations with great cultures designed, and with focused discipline, created the culture. This is because organizations are like gardens. If you do not maintain them, weeds grow. Weeds do not require any human facilitation for growth however; most valuable plants require focused cultivation.

The culture of an organization is based on the values of the organization. These values must be defined if the culture of the organization is to be created by intention.

Organizational vision is what you want to see accomplished in your organization. Organizational mission is what the organization does on a daily basis to see the vision come to pass. Organizational values are what the people of the organization need to be to execute their mission and to see the vision fulfilled. If your focus is only on seeing and doing and not being, you will never obtain what you want to see. A thorough assessment must be done by organizational visionaries of the character values that need to be a reality in the organization for its mission to be executed and for its vision to be realized.

I would use my company as an example. My company has a vision of seeing visionaries of all types and from all cultures be equipped with wisdom to fulfill world changing visions. Our mission is consequently, to provide wisdom, coaching, consulting and curriculums to governments, organizations and leaders to accomplish their world changing visions.

However, as noble as our vision and mission are and as sincere as my wonderful team is, if the values of focused creativity, service, partnership, and synergy are not part of our daily culture, there is no way that vision will be realized or that mission will be executed. Values matter as they are the blocks that make up your culture. The sum total of the values within the organization is your culture. It is easier to create a culture than to reengineer a culture that is an obstacle to the best version of the organization.

Organizational cultural reengineering is a difficult process and certainly not for the faint at heart. This is because people do not change until they have to. Organizational cultural reengineering is like a tooth extraction, it can only be minimized by a good dose of anesthesia. It requires five approaches.

How to Re-engineer a Culture

1. Understand the existing prevailing culture and its origin.

2. Identify all positional and non-positional influences within the company.

3. Create a new code of values with a small team that has been brought into the cultural re-engineering process.

4. Communicate to all influences the new code of values and the reason for the change.

   This could be done in a group setting or one- on-one

depending on the influencer. This stage is the most crucial and will determine whether the cultural change succeeds. It can also be the most painful stage and may in some cases require a CEO to replace key influences that will sabotage the cultural re-engineering process. The influence of people cannot be overlooked in the re-engineering process. The objective of this stage is to have a critical mass of influences within the organization passionately buy into the cultural change and become advocate and messengers of this. If this process is done well, organizational cultural change is possible.

5. Communicate the new code of values to all the staff and create the system for rewarding members of staff who model the required cultural transformation. This is because what gets rewarded gets done.

6. Be a model of the new code of cultural values.

When organizational visionaries do not model the change they want to see in their organizations they lack the moral authority to make it happen.

I once worked as a consultant for a large medical institution. I was brought in to teach customer care. To my horror, during my sessions, I realized that the organization's real cultural values did not support patient care. This was because there was no interdepartmental customer care. The nurses had issues with the doctors and the doctors had issues with the nurses. It was normal for a nurse to ask a nursing assistant from another department to assist with a patient during an emergency and have the nursing assistant say, " it is not possible" because they were not officially supposed to assist that particular nurse.

This led to numerous patient complaints which ended up in the national media. I realized that my efforts to change the culture would have been in vain because the hospital's Board of Director did not have the stomach to endure the painful changes required to bring synergy between the hospital departments with the byproduct of improved patient care.

The Organizational Visionary Exercise:

In reality, what are the existing cultural values of your organization? These may be positive or negative.

List these values.

_____

_____

_____

_____

_____

_____

_____

_____

_____

List an ideal code of values that will support the realization of your vision.

_____

_____

_____

_____

_____

_____

_____

_____

_____

CHAPTER 4

DEFINE THE ORGANIZATIONAL DECISION MAKING MODEL

An organization cannot maintain a level of success that is higher than its quality of decisions.

Every organization has a decision making model whether by design or by default. The effectiveness of this model and the decision makers operating within it, will determine the success of the organization. In creating the decision making model for your organization, it is important to understand which aspects are important to categorize. The operations of organizations are divided into four categories that require different skill sets for good decision making.

These categories are:

1. Strategic Operations
2. Tactical Operations
3. Logistical Operations
4. People Development Operations

There are different types of genetic Intelligences that produce different kinds of leaders. There are strategic leaders, tactical leaders, logistical leaders and diplomatic leaders. Strategic leaders excel at making strategic decision, tactical leaders excel in making tactical decisions, logistical leaders excel in making logistical decisions and diplomatic leaders excel in developing and mediating with people.

Strategic Decision Making

Strategy is a series of sequential steps that takes you from your present reality to your desired future. It sets the vision, mission and creates the path for the organization. It examines its internal and external obstacles and in the business arena, evaluates the impact of the competition. Strategic decision-making must be placed at the helm of the company. An effective decision making model has strategy crafted from the top.

Tactical Decision Making

Tactics is the art of making moves to better ones position in the here and now whether these moves are marketing a product, positioning a service within a market, creating a great presentation, or successfully promoting a product. Defining the aspects of your organization's activities that are tactical and placing your best tactical leaders, managers, and implementers in those roles will enhance your organization. The best sales people are usually tactical.

Logistical Decision Making

Logistics is the procurement, distribution, and management of materials and resources. It is a vital part of any organization. In an army, the generals and war planners create the strategy. The logistical leaders move materials and resources in an organized way to make the strategy happen. The tactical commanders implement the war plan and in the heat of conflict make moves to better their position. Logistical operations cover areas like office administration, accounting and any position related to the management of resources.

Diplomatic or People Development Decision Making

Diplomacy and people development are the backbone of any great organization. This is because you manage materials and lead people. Trying to manage people is an impossible task. It is not an effective approach, as no individual person is identical and every person requires a slightly different approach to ignite their passion and deploy their skills effectively. Diplomatic people make your best human resources consultants, staff and people developers in your organization. They have an innate wisdom to unleash potential in people and mediate and bring harmony among different people.

A great decision model is comprised of three foundations:

1. A clear understanding among all staff of what the vision and yearly strategic goals of the organization are. You cannot make good decisions when the destination of the journey is unknown.

2. A cultural value within the organization that does not allow it to hide from brutal facts. Facing brutal facts whether positive or negative is a must for good decision-making as the quality of your decision is never greater than the quality of your information.

3. Placing your best strategic people in the strategic decision making position, your best tactical people in the tactical decision making areas, your best logistical people in the logistical decision making areas and your best people development and diplomatic decision makers in

the people development area.

I was once the founder and president of a construction company and the strategic aspect of my business involved my associate and me defining the contribution that our construction company can make in an already crowded market. Defining the vision, values mission, and the growth plan of the company, were crucial aspects of managing the implementation of the plan.

Our decision was focused on building maintenance and offered our services to Petrol Stations, which turned out to be very successful. Our logistical operations involved the sourcing and purchasing of raw materials, project management, financial management and quality control.

Our tactical operations involved our maintenance supervisor making decisions on the best way, with excellence and low cost, to provide our clients with the service that they requested on a project-by-project basis. It also involves the sales and promotion of our services to other clients. People-development operations involved our recruiting, retaining and developing construction staff.

Exercise:

Divide and list into the following categories:

1. Strategic Operations – List all the strategic processes within your organization.

_____

_____

_____

_____

_____

_____

_____

_____

_____

_____

_____

_____

_____

_____

_____

_____

2. Tactical Operations – List all the tactical processes within your organization.

_____

_____

_____

_____

_____

_____

_____

_____

_____

_____

_____

_____

_____

_____

_____

_____

3. Logistic Operations – List all the logistic processes within your organization.

_____

_____

_____

_____

_____

_____

_____

_____

_____

_____

_____

_____

_____

_____

_____

_____

_____

4. People-Development Operations – List all the people-development processes within your organization.

_____

_____

_____

_____

_____

_____

_____

_____

_____

_____

_____

_____

_____

_____

_____

_____

_____

_____

5. List the key strategic, tactical, logistical and people-development decision makers in your organization.

_____

_____

_____

_____

_____

_____

_____

_____

_____

_____

_____

_____

_____

_____

_____

_____

_____

_____

CHAPTER 5

DEFINE THE FINANCIAL MODEL THAT DELIVERS THE GREATEST VALUE TO THE ORGANIZATION AND ITS CUSTOMER

Organizations run on a dream fuel called money.

The revenue model of an organization, whether it is a business, a non-for-profit, or government agency, is crucial. It goes without saying that an organization that does not generate enough revenue will be a former organization very soon. Many organizational visionaries in their planning do not spend enough time in researching and creating a sustainable revenue model that reflects market conditions. Let's examine the foundation of a revenue-generating model.

1. Start Up Expense

Every organization requires a certain amount of startup capital. This figure must be accurately calculated and contingencies taken in account.

2. Operating Expense

This is the amount of money that is required to sustain the core operation of the business. It could include premises, salaries and wages of key members of staff, utilities, supplies, insurance, repair and maintenance and miscellaneous expenses.

3. Production Expense

This is the amount of money that is required to produce the products of the organization with excellence and deliver it to the customer in the most efficient way.

4. Income Revenue

This is income that is generated by sales, investment income and in the cases of non-for-profit, grants and donations.

A viable revenue generating model must produce enough finances from income revenue to cover the start-up expenses, operating expenses and production expenses over a period of time and generate a profit.

Exercise:

Develop a sustainable, revenue-generating model for your organization.

List your start up costs.

_____

_____

_____

_____

_____

_____

_____

_____

_____

_____

_____

_____

_____

_____

_____

_____

List your production costs.

_____

_____

_____

_____

_____

_____

_____

_____

_____

_____

_____

_____

_____

_____

_____

_____

List your operating costs.

_____

_____

_____

_____

_____

_____

_____

_____

_____

_____

_____

_____

_____

_____

_____

List your source of income.

PART
TWO

DYNAMICS OF
GREAT
ORGANIZATIONAL
LEADERSHIP

CHAPTER 6

UNDERSTANDING YOUR LEADERSHIP DESIGN

*Organizational leadership is successfully igniting the passion
and deploying the skill of people to accomplish a vision.*

Visionary leadership is the shaping of tomorrow with ideas by working through people. It is the creative force behind organizations that have impacted the world. Vision ignites a leader and the leader then takes that same vision and ignites others to join hand and in hand in shaping the future with that vision. Leading organizations involve igniting people and deploying the skills, passion and character in a strategic way.

Leaders lead best when they lead from their strengths and all comprehensive leadership studies have proven that there is no ideal leadership personality. In my experience, I have found that there are two categories of leaders; habitual leaders and situational leaders. Habitual leaders are those who from leaving the womb seek to set the agenda and create the direction and usually have to learn to follow. Situational leaders are those whose leadership genius only emerges when they are placed in a role that utilizes their gifts and ignites their passion. I have developed a system to help leaders understand their leadership design. I define leadership design as how a person's innate gifts, intelligence, personality, product and interpersonal skills combine to best influence people.

There are three areas that make up a person's leadership design.

A: Leadership intelligence - There are four major areas of leadership intelligence.

1. Strategic Intelligence

Strategy is a series of sequential steps that takes you from your present reality to your desired future. People with strategic intelligence think in patterns, sequences, systems and third, fourth, fifth and sixth order effect. Strategic leaders are the best at creating the strategic plans and leading organizations to achieve strategic objectives.

2. Tactical Intelligence

Tactics is the art of making moves to better ones position in the here and now whether these moves are marketing a product, positioning a service within a market, creating a great presentation or successfully promoting a product. Tactical leaders among other things are the best at promoting and selling goods and services.

3. Logistical Intelligence

Logistics is the procurement, distribution, service, and management of materials and resources. It is a vital part of any organization. Logistical leaders are the best at managing materials and leading administrative systems.

4. Diplomatic Intelligence

Diplomatic Intelligence is the best at developing talents and releasing human potential. These leaders excel at taking people further than they thought they could ever go and achieve more than they ever could. Leaders tend to have a primary intelligence and a secondary intelligence. Studies by David Kieser and Myers Briggs have indicated that these are the following combinations: primary strategic intelligence, secondary diplomatic intelligence; primary diplomatic intelligence and secondary strategic intelligence; primary tactical intelligence, secondary logistical intelligence; primary logistical intelligence, secondary tactical intelligence.

B. Leadership Products

Every great leader has a core product. For Oprah Winfrey, it's inspiring the masses through her talk show. For Warren Buffet, it's as a master investor of other people's money. Of Tiger Woods, it's excellence in the golf course. Of Suzie Orman, it is financial teachings. For Hillary Clinton, it is political expertise. You also have a core product and you lead best when you leverage your expertise and competence in delivering your core product.

C. Leadership Connection

When leaders connect with the heart of followers, anything is possible. The method of connecting with followers, however, will vary from leader to leader based on their design. As I have studied leadership, I have discovered the following primary methods that successful leaders used to connect with followers:

1. Motivation

People follow a leader because he inspires them with his words and actions.

2. Modeling

People follow a leader because of what he represents.

3. Character

People follow the leader because of the depth and greatness of the leader's character. People like Mother Teresa and Nelson Mandella fall into this category.

4. Achievement

People follow a leader because of what he has achieved in the past.

5. Relationship

People follow a leader because of who they know.

6. Development

People follow a leader because the leader brings out the best in them.

7. Experience

People follow a leader because the leader knows more than they do.

8. Opportunity

People follow a leader because the leader gives them access to income and advancement opportunities.

The combination of leadership intelligence, leadership products, and leadership connection creates your leadership design.

Lets look at my leadership design. My leadership intelligence is strategic. My leadership product is that I create organizations, books, programs, seminars, and conferences that impart wisdom to visionaries and I connect with people by developing them. I could be described as a Strategic, Creative and People Development Leader. My former executive assistant is completely different from me. Her intelligence is tactical and her product is promotion and the way she connects with people is through motivation. So, she could be described as a Tactical, Promotional and Motivational Leader.

Exercise:

What is your leadership intelligence?

_____

_____

_____

_____

_____

What is your core leadership product?

_____

_____

_____

_____

_____

How do you connect with follower's heart?

_____

_____

LEADERSHIP DESIGN

_____

_____

_____

CHAPTER 7

UNDERSTANDING THE TALENT, CHARACTER AND PASSION MIX REQUIRED FOR SUCCESS

The complexity and difficulty of fulfilling the vision must determine the talent, character and passion mix of the team.

Every organizational vision requires a unique mixture of talents, passion and character for it to be realized. This mix must be understood. Prudent organizational visionaries count the cost of the human capital required to fulfill the vision. There are three aspects of human capital that must be evaluated.

1. Talent

The competency required in each position of your organization for it to maximize its vision must be understood. A lack of competence in key positions within your organization will lead to disaster. Just as we would not want an incompetent heart surgeon operating on your brother's heart, so must you not allow an incompetent person to operate in your organization.

2. Passion

People excel when placed in roles that they are passionate about. Passion creates pleasure and fulfillment. It causes people to go the second mile. It causes people to work overtime without pay. It is the fountain of all great achievement. Passion causes people to sacrifice today's pleasure for tomorrow's satisfaction. Wise organizational visionaries listen to hear the passion of their staff and discern whether it fits with their company's strategic objectives. If it does, they place them in the roles that they have passion and competence in.

3. Character

Passion and competence, though essential, cannot make up for lack of character. The most dangerous CEO in a company is a passionate competent CEO who is a thief. He would steal with passion and competence and thoroughly cover his tracks. Character is self-leadership. It is the ability to lead oneself to do what is right. Almost everybody knows what is right but not everybody can lead themselves to do what is right. People with high character lead themselves to do what is right even when it is inconvenient. Character is made up of values. A value is a behavior that a person treasures and is not willing to give up easily. These values could be positive or negative. There are positive values like integrity, hard work, creativity, and loyalty that are essential in the building of any great enterprise. An organizational visionary must identify the positive values that are non-negotiable; that they want their leadership team and general staff to have.

During my time spent as a Strategic Consultant to the Probation Department of a particular government, I worked with the Chief Probation Officer whose values were dedication, service, integrity, hard work and authenticity. He however, was surrounded by a significant number of people who shared his vision but whose values were selfishness, gossip, strife, confusion and influencing through chaos. Though well meaning, this dedicated Chief Probation Officer was unable to maximize the potential of his department due to the difference between his values and the key members of his team.

Exercise:

What are the key positions in your organization that you cannot compromise competency in?

_____

_____

_____

_____

_____

_____

_____

_____

What is the passion profile of the people you would want in your organization?

_____

_____

_____

_____

_____

_____

_____

_____

_____

What are the non-negotiable values that you want to see inyour inner circle staff?

_____

_____

_____

_____

_____

_____

_____

_____

What are the nonnegotiable values that you want to see in your general staff?

_____

_____

_____

_____

_____

UNDERSTAND

_____

_____

_____

_____

_____

CHAPTER 8

DEFINE THE PERSONNEL STRUCTURE THAT BEST SUPPORTS THE ACHIEVEMENT OF THE VISION

Organizations behave according to their structure.

The structure of an organization determines how an organization behaves. There is no sacred structure. Structures must be created to maximize the potential of the staff and make prudent decision making easy. There are four major areas in the structure of any organization.

1. The Leadership Structure

Every effective organization must have a primary leader who acts like the captain and steers the ship. Anything with two heads is a monster and anything with three heads is a beast. There must be a clear chain of authority. Within the headship of the organization must abide the authority to create strategy and influence its future. Great leaders, after understanding their design, always staff their weakness. In my organization, because I am a strategic leader, I make sure I surround myself with tactical and logistical leaders.

2. The Management Team

Management is different from leadership. Leadership is about influencing people whereas management is the stewardship of resources to meet preset objectives. An organization with only leaders will break new ground but not maintain its growth. An organization with only managers will be efficient but not break new ground. Leaders shape tomorrow with ideas and managers steward the energies and the resources of the organization to make sure the organization's ideas are implemented.

3. Implementers

Implementers are the heart, soul and wheels of the organization. They deliver the product to the client day in and day out. Leaders create, managers steward their creation, and implementers carry out the work of their creation.

4. Technical Specialists

There are certain organizations that require technical specialists that usually add great value to an organization. These are very skilled and focus- oriented experts in a very specialized area. These specialists vary from industry to industry. An engineering firm's technical specialist will differ from an accounting firm's technical specialist. An example will be a forensic accountant who works is a very specialized accountancy field.

Exercise:

Describe your ideal leadership structure.

_____

_____

_____

_____

_____

_____

_____

_____

_____

Describe your ideal management structure.

_____

_____

_____

_____

_____

_____

_____

_____

Describe your ideal implementation structure.

_____

_____

_____

_____

_____

_____

_____

_____

If required, describe what kind of technical specialist
your organization will need to have.

_____

_____

_____

_____

_____

_____

_____

_____

_____

CHAPTER 9

DESIGN YOUR ORGANIZATIONAL DNA

THE DNA OF YOUR ORGANIZATION

1. THE SOLUTION OF THE ORGANIZATION

The problems the organization solves are:

_____

_____

_____

_____

_____

The solutions the organization serves are:

_____

_____

_____

_____

_____

The market for the solutions the organization serves:

_____

_____

_____

_____

_____

The market for the solutions the organization serves is:

____Increasing
____Stable
____Decreasing

2. THE VISION OF THE ORGANIZATION

The vision of the organization is:

_____

_____

_____

_____

_____

3. <u>THE CULTURE OF THE ORGANIZATION</u>

<u>Define the values that will support the fulfillment of the organizational vision.</u>

_____

_____

_____

_____

_____

_____

_____

_____

4. <u>THE DECISION MAKING MODEL OF THE ORGANIZATION</u>

<u>What are the strategic intensive tasks within the organization?</u>

_____

_____

_____

_____

_____

_____

_____

_____

_____

<u>Who are the best strategic leaders in your organization?</u>

_____

_____

_____

_____

_____

_____

_____

_____

_____

What are the people-development intensive tasks within the organization?

_____

_____

_____

_____

_____

_____

_____

_____

Who are the people-development leaders in your organization?

_____

_____

_____

_____

_____

_____

_____

_____

What are the tactical intensive tasks within the organization?

_____

_____

_____

_____

_____

_____

_____

_____

_____

Who are the best tactical leaders in your organization?

_____

_____

_____

_____

_____

_____

_____

_____

_____

What are the logistical intensive tasks within the organization?

_____

_____

_____

_____

_____

_____

_____

_____

_____

<u>Who are the best logistical leaders in your organization?</u>

_____

_____

_____

_____

_____

_____

_____

_____

_____

5. THE FINANCIAL REVENUE MODEL OF THE ORGANIZATION

What is the average monthly operational expense of the organization?

_____

_____

_____

_____

_____

_____

_____

_____

_____

What is the average monthly production expense of the organization?

_____

_____

_____

_____

_____

_____

_____

_____

_____

What is the average monthly Income revenue of the organization?

_____

_____

_____

_____

_____

_____

_____

_____

_____

6. THE LEADERSHIP APPROACH OF THE CEO AND ITS LEADERSHIP TEAM

What is your leadership intelligence?

_____

_____

_____

_____

_____

_____

_____

_____

_____

What is your core leadership product?

_____

_____

_____

_____

_____

_____

_____

_____

How do you connect with a follower's heart?

_____

_____

_____

_____

_____

_____

_____

_____

_____

1. __THE TYPE OF PEOPLE THE ORGANIZATION ATTRACTS__

Define the talent profile of the team you require to successfully execute the mission of the organization.

_____

_____

_____

_____

_____

_____

_____

_____

_____

Define the passion profile of the team you require to
successfully execute the mission of the organization:

_____

_____

_____

_____

_____

_____

_____

_____

_____

_____

_____

_____

_____

Define the character profile of the team you require to successfully execute the mission of the organization:

_____

_____

_____

_____

_____

_____

_____

_____

_____

_____

_____

_____

7. THE PERSONNEL STRUCTURE OF THE ORGANIZATION

Define your leadership structure.

_____

_____

_____

_____

_____

_____

_____

_____

_____

_____

_____

_____

_____

Define your management structure.

_____

_____

_____

_____

_____

_____

_____

_____

_____

<u>Define your implementation structure.</u>

_____

_____

_____

_____

_____

_____

_____

_____

_____

_____

_____

Define the technical specialist talent required.

_____

_____

_____

_____

_____

_____

_____

_____

_____

8. THE OPERATIONAL SYSTEM OF THE ORGANIZATION

What are the critical transactions or tasks in the organization?

_____

_____

_____

_____

_____

_____

_____

_____

_____

_____

_____

_____

_____

_____

_____

_____

_____

_____

_____

_____

_____

_____

_____

_____

_____

_____

_____

_____

_____

ORGANIZATIONA DNA

_____

_____

_____

_____

_____

_____

_____

_____

_____

_____

_____

_____

_____

_____

THE GIFT OF POLITICAL LEADERSHIP

THE IDEAS AND SOLUTIONS GROUP

Purpose

To equip a critical mass of leaders in nations to bring ideas and solutions from concept to reality through the principles and process of transformational leadership and economic dignity

Vision

To see transformation occur in nations and their economies as leaders emerge who bring ideas and solutions from concept to reality.

Philosophy

1. The problems of a generation will never be greater than the ideas and solutions within people born into that generation
2. These ideas and solutions are within people in the form of an uncommon vision
3. Leadership wisdom is applying principles and taking steps to take ideas and solutions from concept to reality

4. Except the leadership wisdom operating the visionary matches the scope of the vision, the uncommon vision within them will not be fulfilled

About the Author

Andre Thomas is a strategic executive consultant for individuals, businesses, non-profit organizations and governments around the world.

As a writer and coach for visionaries, Andre brings to bear a profound understanding of ancient wisdom on contemporary challenges, to identify and articulate "destiny "DNA"-launching institutions and individuals from the first steps of identifying fundamental strengths, values and goals to accomplished greatness.

As an identity and strategy consultant, Andre has trained hundreds of emerging and renowned business, social, organizational and political leaders. His seminars have included participants from the United Nations, NGOs, government agencies and the private business, education, health and arts/entertainment sectors.

He is the founder and thought leader of The Ideas and Solutions Group

Our website
www.ideasandsolutions.org

OTHER BOOKS
BY ANDRE THOMAS

Unlock Your Greatness (A Young Leaders Handbook)

Uncommon Men and Distinguished Women
(A Rites of Passage Handbook for
Young Men and Women)

The Gift of Organizational Leadership

The Political Visionary

I Am A Leader

www.ingramcontent.com/pod-product-compliance
Lightning Source LLC
Chambersburg PA
CBHW031730210326
41520CB00042B/1653